Angela Cleveland

Also by Angela Cleveland:

I'm No Scaredy Cat... But I'm Afraid to go to School!

Peter's Special Concoction: How a Little Boy Learned to Manage Type 1 Diabetes

Angela Cleveland

The Fruit Files:

Can You Spot the Clues to How These Fruits Feel?

Author: Angela Cleveland

Illustrator: Beth Pierce

Confident Counselor Publishing
13 Tanglewood Court
Monmouth Junction, NJ 08852

Published by Confident Counselor, 13 Tanglewood Court, Monmouth Junction, NJ 08852

ISBN-13: 978-0692837610
ISBN-10: 0692837612

DEDICATION

This book is dedicated to children who struggle with understanding emotions and the families and friends who love them.

CONTENTS

ACKNOWLEDGMENTS

I would like to express my gratitude to my mentors and colleagues in education. As a school counselor, I am blessed to work with a wonderful group of educators who serve as a support system for our students. They foster a positive school climate where all children feel accepted and respected. My students, the dedicated educators I work with, and my school counseling network are a daily inspiration and a constant reminder of the importance of the school counseling profession.

I am especially grateful for the support of my Think Tank co-pilot, grammar guru, and, most importantly, my friend, Mrs. Diane Lyons. It is a rare and treasured gift to find someone who will generously give you honest feedback and guidance.

The Fruit Files: Can You Spot the Clues to How These Fruits Feel?

Cut out this detective's magnifying glass (including the center "glass" area) to closely inspect the Fruit Files.

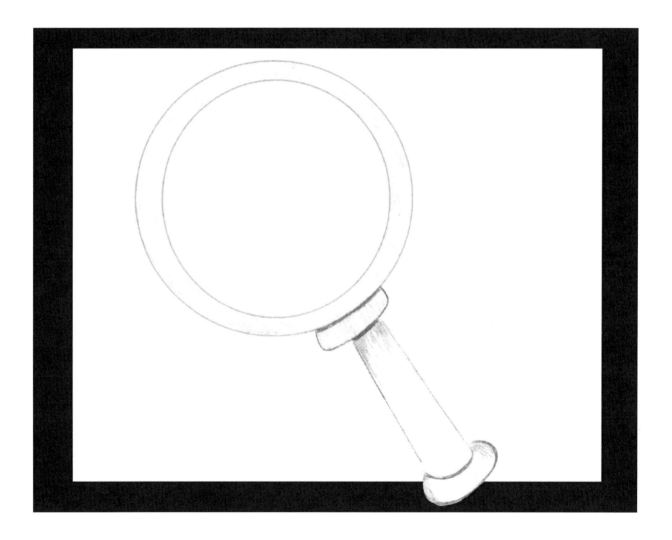

The Fruit Files: Can You Spot the Clues to How These Fruits Feel?

The Fruit Files

Detective _____ **is on the case.**

your name

Investigation opened on _____.

today's date

"It is my business to know things. Perhaps I have trained myself to see what others overlook."

- The Adventures of Sherlock Holmes
by Arthur Conan Doyle

The Angry Apple

Anger is a strong emotion we have when we feel very, very upset. It is a feeling all people have at times. Anger can be an appropriate feeling when we see or experience something upsetting or frustrating. It's important to learn how to manage angry feelings so that we do not say or do something out of anger that can hurt others, ourselves, and our relationships.

Can you spot the clues?

Use your detective's magnifying glass to closely inspect the Angry Apple.

What clues can you find that show the Apple is feeling angry?

Clue 1: _____

Clue 2: _____

Clue 3: _____

Let's reflect!

Think of the last time you were angry. What made you feel so angry? Look in a mirror and make your face look angry.

Are the corners of your mouth pointing up or down?

How do your eyebrows look?

How do your arms and hands look?

When you think back to that time you felt angry, did you say or do something you **wouldn't** have said or done if you were not feeling angry?

List two things you can do to better manage angry feelings:

1. _____

2. _____

Hint: Some kids find it helpful to talk to a trusted adult, listen to music, play with a pet, go for a bike ride, or illustrate their feelings.

The Brave Blackberry

Being brave means that we do not give into fear. It doesn't mean that we are not feeling afraid or worried; it means that we do not let our worries stop us from trying something. It means that we risk failing. We take a deep breath, hold our heads up high, and know that to not try means giving up. We remind ourselves that even if we try and do not succeed, we will still learn something valuable from our experience. So we push ahead, we give 100% effort because we have to – because WE are feeling brave.

Can you spot the clues?

Use your detective's magnifying glass to closely inspect the Brave Blackberry.

What clues can you find that show the Blackberry is feeling brave?

Clue 1: _____

Clue 2: _____

Clue 3: _____

Let's reflect!

Make your brave face! Stand tall. Hold your head up high. Think of how your favorite superhero stands. Stand in the same way he/she stands.

Sometimes you are in new situations or try new things. Some kids say the first day of school or the first time they rode a bike required real bravery. They were nervous and did not know what to expect, but they mustered up their inner superhero. They felt brave!

List two times you had to be brave:

1. _____

2. _____

List one thing you can tell yourself the next time you need to feel brave:

_____

Hint: If you can't think of something you would tell yourself, think of something you would tell a friend or younger sibling.

The Cranky Cantaloupe

When we are feeling annoyed, impatient, or are having an unusually tough day, we are feeling cranky. We all feel cranky from time to time.

Some big triggers for crankiness are being tired, hungry, too hot or too cold. We can also feel this way when something else is bothering us. Sometimes we wake up in a cranky mood, and something that does not typically bother us may contribute to our cranky feeling.

Can you spot the clues?

Use your detective's magnifying glass to closely inspect the Cranky Cantaloupe.

What clues can you find that show the Cantaloupe is feeling cranky?

Clue 1: _____

Clue 2: _____

Clue 3: _____

Let's reflect!

Everyone feels cranky sometimes. Circle the things below that make you feel especially cranky:

hungry   too cold   too quiet   tired

too hot   too noisy   other:

Think of the last time you were cranky. What made you feel cranky?

_____

List two things you can do to help prevent feeling cranky:

1. _____

2. _____

The Guilty Grape

We feel guilty when we have done or said something that goes against our values, what we believe is right or wrong. For example, our values tell us that it is wrong to cheat. If we cheat, we get an uncomfortable feeling in our hearts because we are doing something that goes against our value of being honest.

Can you spot the clues?

Use your detective's magnifying glass to closely inspect the Guilty Grape.

What clues can you find that show the Grape is feeling guilty?

Clue 1: _____

Clue 2: _____

Clue 3: _____

Let's reflect!

Everyone makes mistakes. What does your face look like when you feel guilty? _____

_____

Think of the last time you felt guilty. What happened that made you feel that way? _____

_____

_____

List three trusted adults you can talk to if you have done or said something you feel guilty about:

1. _____

2. _____

3. _____

The Joyful Jackfruit

When we are feeling joyful, we are experiencing great pleasure or happiness. What gives a person the feeling the joy is something unique and special to that person. Big experiences (like a party) can give us joy and so can small, everyday things (like snuggling with a pet).

Can you spot the clues?

Use your detective's magnifying glass to closely inspect the Joyful Jackfruit.

What clues have you found that the Jackfruit is feeling joy?

Clue 1: _____

Clue 2: _____

Clue 3: _____

Let's reflect!

Think of the last time you were VERY happy. Smile! Real smiles are not only seen in your mouth; you can see joy in someone's eyes.

Hold a mirror up to your eyes so that you can see only your eyes. Smile. Frown. How do your eyes look with each expression?

When times are tough, it is especially important to remember the things that bring us joy. These these can be big things (such as a fun school field trip) or small things (like jumping through a big pile of leaves in autumn). Sometimes the small things can give us the greatest joy!

List three things that give you the feeling of joy:

1. _____

2. _____

3. _____

The Kind Kiwi

Kindness involves feeling friendly, generous, and considering the needs of others. When we are feeling kindness to others, it means we go beyond being nice and polite to others. It means that we take action to help someone in need.

Can you spot the clues?

Use your detective's magnifying glass to closely inspect the Kind Kiwi.

What clues can you find that show the Kiwi is feeling kindness to others?

Clue 1: _____

Clue 2: _____

Clue 3: _____

Let's reflect!

Think of the last time you were kind to another person. What did you do?

_____

What did it feel like? _____

Kindness can take place anywhere!

What is one kind thing you can do at school?

_____

What is one kind thing you can do at home?

_____

What is one kind thing you can do in your community?

_____

The Loving Lychee

When we feel love for someone else, we have so many positive feelings for that person that we put their needs before your own at times. We show love by helping others (like cleaning up or helping with homework), doing little things that make them feel special (like tucking them in at night), saying kind words (saying "I love you"), or giving a hug when needed.

Can you spot the clues?

Use your detective's magnifying glass to closely inspect the Loving Lychee.

What clues can you find that show Mama Lychee is feeling love for Baby Lychee?

Clue 1: _____

Clue 2: _____

Clue 3: _____

Let's
reflect!

Think of the last time someone did something loving for you.

What did that person do that let you know he/she loves you? _____

_____

Think of the last time you did something loving for someone else.

What did you do that let that person know you love him/her? _____

_____

List two people who show you that they love you:

1. _____ 2. _____

How do these people let you know that they love you? _____

_____

The Melodramatic Mango

When we are feeling melodramatic, we are expressing emotions or a response that is greatly exaggerated for the situation. Each person experiences a range of emotions for any situation. No two people respond exactly the same way. When we are being melodramatic, our response falls far outside that range of emotions we would expect. Other people who see us might say we are overreacting to situation.

Can you spot the clues?

Use your detective's magnifying glass to closely inspect the Melodramatic Mango.

What clues can you find that show the Mango is feeling Melodramatic?

Clue 1: _____

Clue 2: _____

Clue 3: _____

Let's reflect!

Have you seen someone overreacting to a problem? What did that person do?_____

Circle the melodramatic response to the situation below:

Problem: You can't find your other sock.

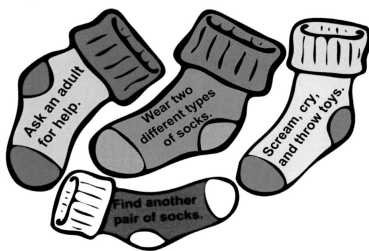

Ask an adult for help.

Wear two different types of socks.

Scream, cry, and throw toys.

Find another pair of socks.

What are the clues you could see in others that let you know that you are having a melodramatic response? _____

The Negative Nectarine

When we are feeling negative, we are only recognizing the bad things. In most situations, there are positive and negative things we can focus on. If we only focus on the bad parts, we are not seeing the whole picture.

Can you spot the clues?

Use your detective's magnifying glass to closely inspect the Negative Nectarine.

What clues can you find that show the Nectarine is being negative?

Clue 1: _____

Clue 2: _____

Clue 3: _____

Let's
reflect!

We all experience negative thoughts that pop into our head. Write down one negative thought you had recently:_____

When these thoughts pop up, we can defeat them with positive words. For example, you can say to yourself, "I'm going to try my best," or, "Even if I don't win, I'm still having fun."

Who is someone you can talk to about how you are feeling?

_____

What is something you can do to lift your mood? (examples: play with a pet, ride your bike, etc...)

_____

_____

The Optimistic Orange

When we are feeling optimistic, we feel a positive sense of hope about the future. We feel confident that we can manage challenges. We can find a lesson learned or something positive in any situation.

Can you spot the clues?

Use your detective's magnifying glass to closely inspect the Optimistic Orange.

What clues can you find that show the Orange is feeling optimistic?

Clue 1: _____

Clue 2: _____

Clue 3: _____

Let's reflect!

Think of the last time you faced a challenge. It could be an academic, athletic, or other challenge.

What positive thoughts did you have during that challenge?

1. _____

2. _____

3. _____

What are three positive things you can tell yourself when facing a challenge so that you can feel optimistic?

1. _____

2. _____

3. _____

The Patient Plum

When we are being patient, it means that we are tolerating (quietly accepting) an uncomfortable situation. We all have to be patient in many situations. Sometimes there are many people waiting in front of us in line. Sometimes we are excitedly waiting for adults to finish a conversation so we can share something. Practicing feeling patient helps us to get along with others.

Can you spot the clues?

Use your detective's magnifying glass to closely inspect the Patient Plum.

What clues can you find that show the Plum is feeling patient?

Clue 1: _____

Clue 2: _____

Clue 3: _____

Let's reflect! 🔍

Think of the last time you had to practice patience.

Where were you? _____

Describe the situation: _____

_____

There are many times when you have to wait your turn, and it can be really hard when you are excited. Some people find that doing something to distract themselves can help pass the time.

What are two things you can do to distract yourself when you have to be patient?

1. _____

2. _____

The Relaxed Raspberry

When we are feeling relaxed, that means we do not have many worries. We do not feel tension in our body or butterflies in our tummy. We all have things we do that we find relaxing.

What is relaxing for one person may not be for another person. For example, some people enjoy quiet time and find that to be relaxing. Others feel that going to a party with lots of people is relaxing.

Can you spot the clues?

Use your detective's magnifying glass to closely inspect the Relaxed Raspberry.

What clues can you find that show the Raspberry is feeling relaxed?

Clue 1: _____

Clue 2: _____

Clue 3: _____

Let's reflect!

Think of the last time you felt relaxed.

Where were you? _____

What were you doing? _____

List two things you can do to relax at home:

1. _____

2. _____

List two things you can do to relax at school:

1. _____

2. _____

The Skeptical Strawberry

When we are feeling skeptical, we do not fully trust the information or the person giving us information. We may doubt the information because it does not sound true to us. We can ask a trusted adult or friend for help deciding if the information is true.

Can you spot the clues?

Use your detective's magnifying glass to closely inspect the Skeptical Strawberry.

What clues can you find that show the Strawberry is feeling skeptical?

Clue 1: _____

Clue 2: _____

Clue 3: _____

Let's reflect!

Think of the last time you felt skeptical. What made you feel that way?

_____

_____

Circle items from the list below that would make you feel skeptical:

On April 1, your sibling tells you the principal has decided that tests are no longer going to be given, so you don't have to study.

While eating dinner, your mom tells you that you have ketchup on your chin.

You are home sick from school. Your best friend calls you after school to tell you that the teacher said there is a math test on Friday.

Who can you talk to if you are feeling skeptical? _____

_____

The Thankful Tomato

When we are feeling thankful, that means that we are feeling happy and grateful for someone or something in our lives. The happiest people are not necessarily those who have a lot of toys. The happiest people are thankful for the things they have and for their family, friends, and other supportive people.

Can you spot the clues?

Use your detective's magnifying glass to closely inspect the Thankful Tomato.

What clues have you found that the Tomato is feeling thankful?

Clue 1: _____

Clue 2: _____

Clue 3: _____

Let's
reflect!

What are you thankful for at school? _____

What are you thankful for at home? _____

What are you thankful for in your community? _____

List three things you were thankful for in the past week:

1. _____

2. _____

3. _____

The Wishy-Washy Watermelon

When we are feeling wishy-washy, we are having a hard time making a decision. Some decisions can be difficult because we have to choose from many good things. For example, there may be several games you can play at recess, but you only have a short period of time and have to pick one game. When we are feeling wishy-washy, it can feel impossible to make a decision.

Can you spot the clues?

Use your detective's magnifying glass to closely inspect the Wishy-Washy Watermelon.

What clues can you find that show the Watermelon is feeling wishy-washy?

Clue 1: _____

Clue 2: _____

Clue 3: _____

Let's
reflect!

Think of the last time you had a hard time making a decision.

What was the decision? _____

_____

How did you decide? _____

_____

Everyone struggles with decisions at times. From the list below, circle what you would do to help you with a tough decision:

talk to a
friend

write a
pro/con list

talk to an
adult

other:
_____

The Fruit Files: Can You Spot the Clues to How These Fruits Feel?

Evidence Log

The Angry Apple

arms are crossed

frowning

eyebrows pointed in and down

scared apples nearby

The Brave Blackberry

smiling

giving thumbs up

saying encouraging words

standing tall

The Cranky Cantaloupe

clenching fists

crying loudly

tears

Evidence Log

Evidence Log

### The Guilty Grape 	looking around mouth is tense behavior – changing a grade
### The Joyful Jackfruit 	smiling waving arms behavior – doing a fun activity
### The Kind Kiwi 	smiling observing friend needed help – looking at dropped book behavior – helping to pick up a dropped book

Evidence Log

The Loving Lychee

Baby Lychee smiling

Mama Lychee smiling

behavior - Mama Lychee taking care of Baby Lychee even she is in the middle of ironing

The Melodramatic Mango

crying

yelling

family surprised by reaction (mouth open in O shape)

behavior – overreacting to lost sock

The Negative Nectarine

mouth turned down in frown

thinking the team will lose

behavior – standing with shoulders slumping

Evidence Log

The Optimistic Orange

smiling

thinking positive thoughts

behavior - standing in confident, superhero posture

The Patient Plum

situation – long line for ice cream

distracting oneself from long line with fun activity

smiling

The Relaxed Raspberry

smiling

doing relaxing activity

eyes are partly closed

feet up in relaxed posture

Evidence Log

The Skeptical Strawberry

arms crossed

looking sideways

frowning

The Thankful Tomato

smiling

thinking grateful thoughts

behavior – cleaning up toys and not complaining about doing a chore

The Wishy-Washy Watermelon

scratching head

eyes are wide, worried

frowning

behavior - not responding to friend with an answer

About the Author

Angela Cleveland has been a professional school counselor/anti-bullying specialist since 2001. Angela co-founded ReigningIt (www.ReigningIt.com), "creating a #STEM dialogue inclusive of every woman."

Angela is the author of

- *The Fruit Files: Can You Spot the Clues to How These Fruits Feel?*
- *I'm No Scaredy Cat...But I'm Afraid to go to School!*
- *Peter's Special Concoction: How a Little Boy Learned to Manage Type 1 Diabetes*

Learn more about Angela. Follow her on Twitter (@AngCleveland) and visit: www.AngelaCleveland.com.

About the Illustrator

Beth Pierce is an office worker by day, freelance cartoonist by night. She lives in New Jersey with her husband, daughter and two crazy cats. Beth's artwork can be found on Instagram (instagram.com/littlebchan) and Tumblr (littlebchan.tumblr.com).

Made in the USA
Lexington, KY
28 May 2018